A Little Jewish Cookbook

Barbara Bloch

ILLUSTRATED BY FIONA LEIBOWITZ

First published in 1989 by
Appletree Press Ltd, 7 James Street South,
Belfast BT2 8DL.
Text © Barbara Bloch, 1989.
Illustrations © Fiona Leibowitz, 1989.
Printed in China. All rights reserved.

First published in the United States in 1989
by Chronicle Books, 275 Fifth Street,
San Francisco, California 94103.

ISBN 0-87701-700-X

9 8 7 6 5 4

A note on measures
Spoonfuls and dry cup measures are level
unless otherwise stated.

Introduction

Jewish cooking is not necessarily kosher food cooked according to ancient religious dietary laws, nor is it a new cuisine from the modern state of Israel. Rather it is a centuries-old cuisine with an international flavor that reflects the multi-national backgrounds of the Jewish people. I would be surprised to find two Jewish cooks who would prepare any recipe in exactly the same way. Most cooks have their own versions of recipes, often based on memories of "the way Mama cooked". Few things reflect Jewish cooking and temperament more than individuality and the conviction that cooking for someone is a special gift of love.

For those readers who are kosher, you will find a kosher option within every recipe that is not kosher. For those readers who are not Jewish, but have always assumed that meat and dairy products are never combined in Jewish cooking, it should be noted that, while this was more or less true up until the middle of the nineteenth century, today ancient dietary laws are observed primarily by Orthodox Jews. The majority of Jewish homes are neither Orthodox nor kosher and, in those homes, it is not at all uncommon to find butter served at every meal and coffee served regularly with milk or cream, even when the main course is a thick juicy steak.

Scrambled Eggs and Lox

Breakfast in most Jewish homes from Monday to Friday is just like frantic breakfasts everywhere else in the western world. Weekends however, are likely to be a very different matter: fresh bagels with cream cheese and lox (smoked salmon); herring in cream sauce or smoked whitefish from the delicatessen; sometimes Blintzes (see page 6); or Scrambled Eggs and Lox, served with toasted bagels, rye bread, or challah. If you're worried about calories, sleep late on the weekend. This way you avoid temptation!

8 eggs
I small onion, diced
freshly ground pepper to taste
4 oz lox, diced
4–6 tbsp butter
freshly chopped parsley to garnish
(serves 4)

Beat eggs in bowl with pepper and 2 tbsp water. Set aside. Melt butter in skillet (frying pan), add onion, and cook until transparent. Add lox and cook, stirring, for about 2 minutes. Add beaten eggs to skillet and cook over low heat, stirring constantly, until eggs are set. Spoon onto serving dishes and garnish with parsley.

Note It isn't necessary to add salt to eggs because smoked salmon is salty. How salty it is depends on what kind you buy: lox, Nova Scotia, Scotch, Irish or Norwegian to name but a few. Wouldn't you know, my favorite is Scotch salmon which is also the most expensive.

Cheese Blintzes

A "crêpe" by any other name — palatschinken, blini, egg roll, pfannkuchen, enchilada, crespelle, thin pancake, or blintz — all start out very much the same way but end up as though they weren't related at all! Blintzes are Jewish crêpes, filled with cheese or fruit, fried, and served with sour cream and/or jam for breakfast or lunch. They can be bought frozen, ready to cook, but they're better made from scratch. Fry them immediately or freeze them and fry them (without defrosting) whenever you have the urge to eat a blintz, or you have to feed last minute (or worse still, uninvited) guests.

I container (I lb) farmer or cottage cheese
I egg yolk, beaten
2 tbsp sugar
grated rind of I lemon
I tbsp melted butter
$1/2$ tsp vanilla (optional)
18 to 20 crêpes (each 6 inch), cooked on I side only
unsalted butter for frying
dairy sour cream and/or jam to serve
(serves 6)

Place first 6 ingredients in bowl and mix until well combined. Spoon I heaping tbsp filling onto center of uncooked side of each crêpe. Fold crêpes in slightly on opposite ends, then fold in on sides to make rectangular envelopes. Melt butter in skillet (frying pan) and fry filled blintzes, seam side down, until lightly browned. Turn over and brown on other side. Serve warm with sour cream and/or jam.

Bread

What a shock it would be to be served presliced, packaged, preservative-filled, supermarket bread instead of freshly baked French bread in a French home. It is an unlikely scenario. Jewish homes also have special bread. Most popular is fresh Jewish rye, with or without caraway seed, sometimes with onion. Other typical Jewish breads include dark, black pumpernickel, plain or bursting with raisins; corn bread, heavy and moist on the inside, crisp on the outside; bagels, those crazy doughnut-shaped rolls; and challah, a Sabbath bread made with white flour, eggs, and sugar, with or without poppy, sesame, or fennel seed on top, shaped into a thick or round twist. Freshly sliced and served with sweet butter or cream cheese, these breads are truly special.

Years ago I took a sandwich order to a local delicatessen for some people with whom I worked. One order was for chopped chicken liver on white bread. The delicatessen owner was so horrified that he refused to take the order, and I couldn't blame him! If a Jewish family lives in an area where good Jewish rye bread is not available (and there are many), they usually are more than willing to drive many miles to buy it. The only food I take with me on our annual summer vacation is bread. And when guests ask what they can bring, the answer is always the same: "Fancy gifts we don't need, but if you want good sandwiches, bring fresh rye bread. It's the only important food we can't buy on the island."

Schmaltz and Griebens

The special flavor of Schmaltz (rendered chicken fat) is as intrinsic to good Jewish cooking as olive oil is to Italian cooking. The main difference is that olive oil is considered healthy while chicken fat decidedly is not. The use of chicken fat presents exactly the same dilemma as the use of bacon fat — it isn't good for you, but it certainly adds a special flavor to food. (Why should it be that "if it tastes good it's bad for you"?) Several recipes in this book call for schmaltz. Its use is entirely optional. If you're on a restricted low fat, low cholesterol diet don't use it. But if you're healthy, a little schmaltz now and then on special occasions won't kill you. You can buy it at some supermarkets, but don't. Make it at home and save money. Whenever you clean a chicken, remove the excess fat and place it in a container in the freezer. When you have about a pound of fat, render it as follows:

Place chicken fat in deep, heavy saucepan. If desired, cut some fatty chicken skin into small pieces and add to pan. Cover with water, bring to a boil, cover pan, reduce heat, and cook until most of the water has evaporated. Uncover pan and cook until nothing remains in pan but rendered chicken fat and small pieces of skin. Add diced onion and cook, uncovered, until skin (called griebens) is crisp and onion is lightly browned. Strain fat and store it in container in freezer or refrigerator. Serve griebens and onion on matzo or thick slices of bread.

Cucumber · Fennel · Yogurt Salad

On a hot summer day, when I am feeling too hot and lazy to cook, I mix equal amounts of cottage cheese and dairy sour cream in a bowl and stir in diced cucumber, green pepper, and radishes. With a few slices of buttered rye bread I have the perfect lunch to take out on the terrace. But, if I am making salad for company, something a bit more festive is called for. If you serve this salad with cold sliced meat or smoked fish and tomato slices, fresh from the garden, you can still avoid cooking, or at least the kind of cooking that makes you and the kitchen hot.

I large cucumber, peeled and thinly sliced,
as many seeds removed as possible
salt
I clove garlic, crushed
2 fennel bulbs, thinly sliced
I container (I lb) plain yogurt
freshly chopped mint leaves to garnish
(serves 4)

Place prepared cucumbers in bowl and sprinkle with salt. Cover cucumbers with plate and place weight on plate. Set aside for about 30 minutes. Drain liquid from cucumbers and place drained cucumbers and fennel in large bowl. Stir gently to mix. Stir garlic into yogurt. Spoon yogurt over vegetables and toss gently to coat. Spoon into salad bowl and garnish with mint.

Felafel with Tachina

Felafel is Middle Eastern "street food" wildly popular in Israel where it is sold at corner kiosks. You can increase or decrease seasoning as you wish. Devoted Felafel fans like it as hot as possible. Tachina (sesame sauce) can be made at home but is also available in many supermarkets.

I can (I lb) chick-peas, drained
2 cloves garlic
I onion
2–3 tbsp freshly chopped parsley
I egg
I tsp ground cumin
¹/₄ tsp coriander seed
¹/₈ tsp cayenne
salt and freshly ground pepper to taste

---

8 tbsp bulgur (cracked wheat), soaked I hour and drained
flour
vegetable oil for deep frying
pita bread and tachina (sesame sauce) to serve
(serves 8)

Place first 9 ingredients in food processor and process to smooth paste. Add bulgur and process until mixture forms large ball. Flour hands and form into I inch balls. Heat 3 inches of oil in deep, heavy saucepan to 375°F. Drop balls into hot oil and fry until crisp and dark brown. Remove with slotted spoon and drain on paper towels. Serve in pita pockets and spoon tachina over.

Sautéed Chicken Livers
with Artichoke Hearts

Chicken livers aren't always chopped! Sautéed livers are wonderful with eggs. Add vegetables and they're great for lunch. You can even serve them for dinner. A dear friend periodically reminds me of a dinner party I gave many years ago and, lacking money for a fancy roast, I served chicken livers. Older and wiser now, I'd worry that perhaps someone wouldn't like them. But everyone ate them then, and my friend still remembers them as delicious and original — which should tell me something positive about the courage of youth.

---

4 tbsp schmaltz or butter
I onion, sliced
I pkg (9 oz) frozen artichoke hearts, thawed
***or** I lb sliced button mushrooms*
I clove garlic, minced
I lb chicken livers, rinsed, trimmed and halved
$1/2$ cup chicken stock or broth
4 tbsp Marsala
salt and freshly ground pepper to taste
toast triangles or mashed potatoes to serve
(serves 4)

Melt schmaltz in large skillet (frying pan), add onion and artichoke hearts, and cook until onion is transparent. Add garlic and chicken livers. Cook for 5 to 6 minutes or until livers are browned. Remove from pan, pour chicken stock and Marsala into skillet, and scrape up pan juices over high heat.

Season with salt and pepper and pour over livers. Serve over toast triangles or with mashed potatoes.

Chopped Herring

Chopped Herring can be served as an hors d'oeuvre spread on cocktail bread, crackers, or small matzo. It can also be served as a first course, on a bed of lettuce. Herring, in endless forms, is almost basic to Jewish cuisine. If you want to serve herring as an hors d'oeuvre without having to actually cook, just buy three or four different kinds of imported herring fillets in a good delicatessen, cut the herring into small pieces and serve with toothpicks and lots of napkins to catch the drips.

---

2 hard-cooked eggs
l jar (l lb) matjes herring, drained
l large onion
l large, tart apple, peeled and cored
l thick slice white bread, crusts removed, soaked in red wine
vinegar and squeezed dry
l tbsp sugar or to taste
salt and freshly ground pepper to taste
(makes about 3 cups)

Finely chop l egg and set aside. Place remaining ingredients in food processor and process just until all ingredients are chopped. Spoon into serving bowl. Sprinkle reserved chopped egg on top. Serve as suggested above.

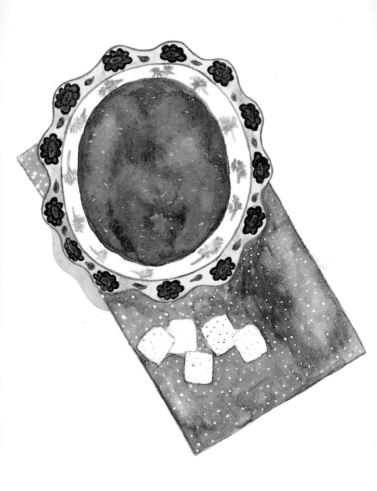

Chopped Chicken Liver Pâté

This is an all-time favorite, served as an hors d'oeuvre with crackers or as a sandwich, spread on rye bread and topped with slices of raw onion. It was a French chef who taught me to flavor the liver with Madeira or sweet sherry, rather than with brandy, as a way to eliminate the slightly bitter flavor livers sometimes have. If you don't want to use Madeira, try a pinch of sugar instead.

---

4 tbsp schmaltz or butter
1 onion, finely chopped
2 cloves garlic, minced
1 lb chicken livers, rinsed, trimmed, and halved
salt and freshly ground pepper to taste
2 hard-boiled eggs, cut into chunks
2 tbsp Madeira or to taste
parsley sprigs to garnish
cocktail bread, crackers, or small round matzo to serve
(makes about 2 cups)

Melt schmaltz in skillet (frying pan), add onion, and cook until transparent. Add livers, garlic, salt, and pepper to skillet, and sauté until livers are thoroughly cooked. Spoon entire contents of skillet into food processor or blender. Add eggs and Madeira and process for about 1 minute or until blended but not smooth. Adjust seasoning. Spoon into serving dish and smooth top. Cover and refrigerate until chilled. To serve, garnish with parsley sprigs and surround with cocktail bread, crackers, or small round matzo.

Gefilte Fish

Gefilte fish is nothing more or less than fish quenelles. If you make tiny fish balls you can serve them as an hors d'oeuvre. If the balls are large, they are usually served as a first course, always with prepared horseradish.

---

3 lb white fish fillets (combination of carp, whitefish, pike),
heads and bones reserved
sliced onion, carrot, celery, and parsley for stock
2 eggs
1 onion, grated
4 tbsp dry bread crumbs or matzo meal
$^1/_4$ tsp ground nutmeg (optional)
salt and freshly ground pepper to taste
sliced, cooked carrots and prepared horseradish to serve
(makes about 24 large patties)

Place fish heads and bones in large, heavy stockpot with stock ingredients and fill pot with water. Bring to a boil. Place fish fillets, eggs, grated onion, bread crumbs, nutmeg, salt, and pepper in food processor and process until smooth. Wet hands with cold water and form fish mixture into oval patties or small balls. Add to stockpot, reduce heat, and simmer for $1^1/_2$ to 2 hours (stock should be reduced by half). Remove fish with slotted spoon and set aside to cool. Strain stock and refrigerate (it will jell). Refrigerate patties until well chilled. Serve patties with small amount of jellied sauce, an attractively cut slice of carrot, and prepared horseradish. Serve tiny balls with toothpicks and horseradish.

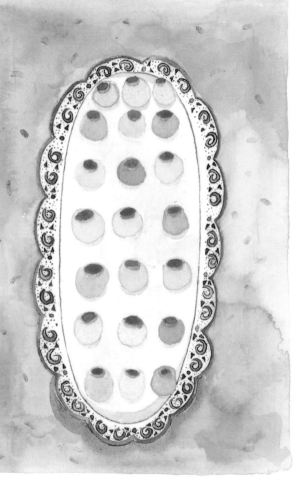

Chicken Soup

Well flavored, homemade chicken soup is very much the same the world over. It is basic to Jewish cooking because of its perceived healing qualities. Maybe calling chicken soup "Jewish penicillin" isn't so dumb. After all, when chicken soup is made specially for someone who is ill, it is an act of love — and love and concern can be the best medicine in the world.

Start by making good chicken stock. If you can find stewing (boiling) chicken, use it. Otherwise use any chicken. Place in large stock pot and fill pot with cold water. Cut up onions, carrots, and celery and add to pot with garlic and fresh parsley. If you have a turnip or parsnip, add them too — it couldn't hurt. Add kosher salt to taste if you have it; add regular salt if you don't. Bring to a rapid boil and skim off foam and all traces of fat. Reduce heat, add peppercorns, cover, and cook for several hours. Continue to skim off fat as it rises to surface and add more water if necessary.

When stock is ready, remove chicken and set aside. Strain stock and place in clean saucepan to use as base for chicken soup. Now you're on your own! Add anything you want: diced, cooked chicken; cooked noodles or other pasta; cooked rice or barley; shredded or diced, cooked carrots; cooked peas; whatever you have on hand.

If you have made more stock than you need for soup, place extra stock in containers in freezer and use next time you have a sick friend or whenever a recipe calls for chicken stock.

Mushroom and Barley Soup

If you use homemade beef stock, make it with a small piece of brisket and add diced meat to the soup for a hearty winter dish. And, if your sick friend is getting better (see Chicken Soup, page 25), add a little variety to your "good deed" and take Mushroom and Barley Soup instead of Chicken Soup.

---

4 tbsp butter
I onion, chopped
I stalk celery, diced
I carrot, diced
8 cups stock or broth (beef, chicken, or vegetable)
$^1/_2$ cup pearl barley, rinsed and picked over
salt and freshly ground pepper to taste
I lb button mushrooms, sliced
I container (8 oz) dairy sour cream
freshly chopped parsley to garnish
(serves 6)

Melt 2 tbsp butter in skillet (frying pan) and sauté onion, celery, and carrot. Set aside. Place stock in large heavy saucepan, add barley, sautéed onion, celery, carrot, salt, and pepper. Bring to a boil, reduce heat, cove;, and simmer until barley is tender, about I hour. Melt remaining 2 tbsp butter in skillet and sauté mushrooms. Add mushrooms to soup and stir in sour cream. Cook over low heat just until heated through. Adjust seasoning. Spoon into soup bowls and garnish with parsley.

Cold Beet Borscht

There are three ways to make this. Start from scratch with fresh beets, use canned beets, or buy a jar of borscht and doctor it up. There's very little difference in borscht made from fresh or canned beets, but ready-made borscht is easy to spot, even if you got a medical degree before you did the doctoring. There are lots of things I'd rather do with my time than try to impress people with nice evenly cut julienne strips, so I use canned beets.

---

2 cans (1 lb each) julienne beets
beef stock or broth
4 tbsp fresh lemon juice
1 onion, grated
2 tbsp sugar
salt to taste
2 eggs
8 hot, peeled, boiled potatoes to serve
dairy sour cream to serve
(serves 8)

Drain beet juice into large measuring cup. Place beets in saucepan. Add enough stock to beet juice to make 10 cups. Pour into saucepan. Add lemon juice, onion, sugar, and salt. Bring to a boil, reduce heat, and simmer for 20 minutes. Beat eggs in large bowl. Pour small amount of soup slowly into beaten eggs, beating constantly to keep eggs from curdling. Pour remaining soup into egg mixture, beating constantly. Place in refrigerator until well chilled. Serve in large soup bowls with boiled potatoes and generous dollops of sour cream.

Matzo Stuffing

Passover is a celebration of The Exodus of the Jews from Egypt when everyone had to leave in such a hurry that they didn't have time to let their bread rise. It begins with a big dinner – actually two dinners on successive nights in case historians got the original date wrong! The dinners are called Seders, which is what da Vinci painted in *The Last Supper*. Seders are ritual dinners everyone attends, even relatives you don't particularly like, and good friends, whether or not they're Jewish. Turkey or roast chicken is often served, but during Passover, in remembrance of the bread that didn't have time to rise, nobody eats leavened bread, or leavened anything. Since you can't make bread stuffing you could use rice instead, but matzo (flat pieces of unleavened bread) is better.

---

10 to 12 broken matzo
2 cups chicken stock or broth
1 egg, beaten
2 tbsp schmaltz, margarine, or vegetable oil
turkey or chicken giblets, cooked and chopped
$^{1}/_{2}$ lb sliced button mushrooms, sautéed
1 stalk celery, chopped and sautéed
1 large onion, chopped and sautéed
$^{1}/_{2}$ cup slivered almonds
freshly chopped parsley
salt and freshly ground pepper to taste
(makes 8 or 9 cups)

Combine all ingredients in large bowl and mix well. Stuff turkey or chickens, *just before roasting*.

Matzo Ball Soup

Matzo Ball Soup, a tradition at Passover, has its own special memory for our family. We had an Aunt Mabel who, during her lifetime, was the moving spirit behind our Seders. She loved to cook, and matzo balls were her specialty. In spite of the fact that, in her later years, her hearing and eyesight were very poor, she absolutely refused to allow anyone else to make the matzo balls. She would break the eggs into a bowl, and, invariably, small amounts of egg shell would fall into the bowl too. She never noticed, and we didn't have the heart to tell her. But every Passover, without fail, someone will mention how much they miss the egg shells in our matzo balls — or in truth, how much we all miss Aunt Mabel.

---

1 tbsp freshly chopped parsley
¼ tsp ground ginger (optional)
salt and freshly ground pepper to taste
4 tbsp melted schmaltz or vegetable oil
½ cup sparkling water
1 cup matzo meal
4 eggs, beaten
Chicken Soup (see page 25)
(makes about 24 balls)

Stir parsley, ginger, salt, and pepper into schmaltz. Add eggs and sparkling water and beat to blend. Stir in matzo meal (mixture should be moist). Refrigerate for 1 hour. Wet hands and form into walnut-sized balls. Drop into boiling soup. Reduce heat, cover, and simmer for 20 minutes or until balls float to top. Serve in soup, 2 to 3 balls per serving.

Charoseth

Charoseth is a symbolic food served at a Seder and during the week of Passover. It is a mixture that symbolizes the mortar used by the Jewish slaves in Egypt to build monuments for their masters. The sweetness in it symbolizes the joy of hard-won freedom when they fled (with their unleavened bread). Charoseth is made with fresh and/or dried fruit, nuts, cinnamon, sugar, and red wine. But it makes absolutely no difference what kind of fruit or nuts you use. Just mix everything together, season to taste, and add the wine. Spread it on matzo and eat it carefully. Charoseth tends to fall off the matzo — usually on your best silk dress or tie! This is one of many dishes always served at Passover, but it can be served at any time of year.

Basic mixture
2 apples, finely chopped
1 cup coarsely chopped walnuts
2 tbsp grated lemon rind — more if desired
2 tsp cinnamon, or to taste
sugar to taste
enough red wine to bind mixture together
If desired, add or substitute: chopped dates, figs, or apricots;
raisins; small banana chunks; a little orange juice; other kinds
of nuts; ground nutmeg; freshly grated ginger; honey
(makes 2 to 3 cups)

Mix everything together, place in attractive bowl, and chill until ready to serve.

Sweet and Sour Pot Roast

Don't invite too many people for dinner! Leftover cold pot roast makes wonderful sandwiches, served on rye bread of course.

3-4 lb boneless brisket of beef .
4 cups beef stock
2 cups dry red wine
I large onion, sliced
I clove garlic, minced
2 tbsp brown sugar
3 tbsp ketchup
salt to taste
cooked noodles or Potato Latkes (see page 45),
applesauce, and vegetable to serve
(serves 6—8)

Trim meat of excess fat. Brown meat well on both sides under broiler (grill). Place next 7 ingredients in large heavy saucepan. Stir until well combined. Add meat, cover, and cook over low heat until meat is very tender, 2 $\frac{1}{2}$ to 3 hours, turning meat over from time to time. If necessary, add additional liquid during cooking. When meat is tender, remove from pan and keep warm. Taste cooking liquid and adjust seasoning, if necessary. If desired, cook liquid, uncovered, until slightly reduced, but do not thicken with flour. Gravy should be thin but well flavored. Slice meat and serve with hot cooked noodles, applesauce, and vegetable. Spoon gravy over meat and noodles.

Tongue with Raisin Sauce

Either you like tongue or you don't. If you do like it, you'll find it's really special when served with raisin sauce. We like tongue and serve it fairly often, sometimes plain with sharp mustard and sometimes with this sauce that my grandmother used to make. She always served tongue with spinach and mashed potatoes. Old habits die hard, so I do too. Even if we didn't like tongue we'd have to buy it anyway — our dog has a passion for it and, after all, he's part of the family too!

---

8 tbsp dark brown sugar
1 tbsp all-purpose (plain) flour
1 tsp dry mustard
2 tbsp fresh lemon juice
2 tbsp cider vinegar
1/2 cup raisins
1/2 tsp grated lemon rind
salt and freshly ground pepper to taste
1 cooked tongue, peeled and thinly sliced
(makes 2 1/2 cups sauce)

Place sugar, flour, and mustard in saucepan and stir to combine. Pour 1 1/2 cups water into saucepan, stirring to dissolve sugar. Stir in lemon juice, vinegar, raisins, and lemon rind. Bring to a boil, stirring constantly. Reduce heat and cook until sauce thickens. Season with salt and pepper. Serve hot over hot, sliced tongue.

Note Cold tongue, like cold pot roast, makes wonderful sandwiches. Make your sandwiches with mustard, lettuce, and — you guessed it — fresh rye bread.

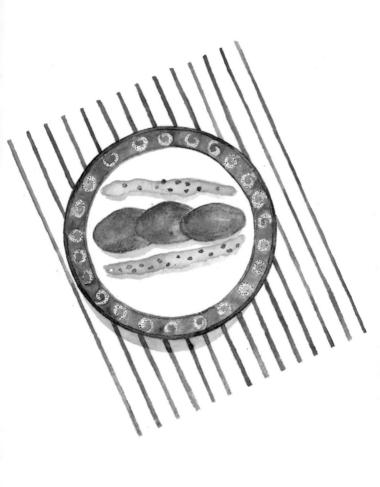

Lamb Eggplant Casserole

Cumin provides a nice Middle Eastern flavor. But, if you don't like the flavor of cumin, substitute dill, mint, basil, or even curry. If possible, make this one day ahead to give the flavors time to get acquainted.

---

1 lb lean ground lamb
2 tsp ground cumin or to taste
salt and freshly ground pepper to taste
olive oil for cooking
2 onions, chopped
1 large eggplant (aubergine), peeled and cubed
3 cups tomato sauce (puréed tomatoes)
2 cans (6 oz each) pitted black olives
8 oz feta cheese, crumbled (optional)
finely crushed cracker crumbs or matzo for topping
(serves 6)

Preheat oven to 350°F. Brown meat in large skillet (frying-pan) and season with cumin, salt, and pepper. Place in colander to drain off fat and spoon into large bowl. Wipe out skillet. Heat about 2 tbsp olive oil in skillet, add onions, and cook until transparent. Stir into meat and set aside. Add additional olive oil to skillet and sauté eggplant cubes until browned. Spread tomato sauce over bottom of casserole. Cover with half of meat-onion mixture, add layer of half of eggplant cubes, and sprinkle half of olives and half of cheese over. Cover with tomato sauce and repeat layers, ending in tomato sauce. Sprinkle crushed cracker crumbs over top. Bake for 30 to 45 minutes or until heated through. Serve with tossed green salad.

Noodle Kugel

Noodle Kugel is simply noodle pudding. It doesn't have to be sweet, but it usually is. Sweet Kugel is served as an accompaniment to a main dish or as dessert. It can be made with or without cheese, or with or without fruit. One big advantage to a Kugel is that it can be made ahead of time and baked immediately prior to serving. My idea of the perfect dinner party is a menu where as much as possible is cooked in advance and then heated in the oven while I sit in the living room with my guests and act as though I don't have a culinary thought on my mind. But even if no one is fooled by my pretense, it cuts down on the after dinner clean up!

I lb broad egg noodles, cooked, drained, and still hot
$^1/_2$ cup butter, cut into small pieces
4 eggs, beaten
8 tbsp sugar
4 tbsp raisins
I jar (8 oz) applesauce
I can (I lb) crushed pineapples, drained
I jar (10 oz) apricot preserves
(serves 6–8)

Preheat oven to 350°F. Toss hot noodles with butter to coat. Combine next 5 ingredients and beat until well mixed. Add to noodles and toss gently. Spoon into a greased casserole dish, and smooth top. Spread preserves over noodles and bake for about 45 minutes or until top is browned. Serve hot.

Latkes

If you make Latkes (Potato Pancakes) the day you plan to serve them, you had better hope your guests think the smell of Latkes cooking is perfumed air. But, if you would rather not have your guests sniff the air as they arrive and announce "Oh my — Latkes for dinner!" then make them ahead of time, freeze them, and reheat in the oven just before serving. I spent an entire day making little Latkes with a friend to serve at the wedding of one of my daughters. Fortunately we made them ahead of time, because it took days to get the smell out of the house. Clearly, weddings should not smell of Latkes — flowers are better!

---

6 medium-sized potatoes
1 onion, grated
2 eggs, beaten
3 tbsp matzo meal or all-purpose (plain) flour
salt and freshly ground pepper to taste
schmaltz or butter for frying
applesauce, dairy sour cream, and/or caviar to serve
(makes about 18 large pancakes)

Peel and grate potatoes and place in large bowl of ice-water to keep them from turning brown. Squeeze dry and place in dry bowl. Add onion, eggs, matzo meal, salt, and pepper. Mix well. Heat schmaltz in skillet (frying pan) and drop mixture into skillet in large or small spoonfuls depending on size of Latke desired. Brown well on both sides and drain on paper towels. Serve small Latkes hot as appetizers with applesauce, sour cream, and/or caviar. Serve large Latkes with applesauce as an accompaniment to the main dish.

Sweet and Sour Red Cabbage

There are very few things about which my husband and I disagree strongly, but cabbage is one of them. I've resolved the problem by simply not cooking cabbage for him — ever! As a result, my heart leaps for joy whenever I spot red cabbage on a menu, and you may be certain I order it. This recipe is one of my favorites.

I large red cabbage, shredded (about I 1/2 lbs)
2 firm tart apples, peeled, cored, and diced
I tbsp all-purpose (plain) flour
4 tbsp red wine vinegar
I 1/2 tbsp sugar or to taste
2 tbsp melted schmaltz or butter
salt and freshly ground pepper to taste
(serves 6)

Place cabbage and apples in I cup lightly salted water. Cover and cook for I5 minutes. Stir flour into vinegar until smooth. Add sugar and stir well. Pour over cabbage. Add schmaltz, salt, and pepper. Stir well, cover, and cook over low heat for I5 minutes or until cabbage is tender.

Vegetable · Fruit Tzimmes

Before you cook a Tzimmes, you should know what it is. But every definition is different! Some books say a Tzimmes is "something special" — but that depends on what a person thinks is special. Some say it's sweet — but lots of things are sweet that aren't a Tzimmes. Most recipes have carrots — but not all. You can make a Tzimmes with or without meat, use potatoes (sweet or white), carrots, apples, prunes, apricots, or other food, in just about any combination. So what is a Tzimmes? See above!

---

3 large carrots, thickly sliced
3 yams or sweet potatoes, peeled and thickly sliced
$^1/_2$ lb pitted prunes, soaked until softened
3 Granny Smith apples, peeled and thickly sliced
8 tbsp brown sugar
salt and freshly ground pepper to taste
3 tbsp schmaltz or butter
(serves 6)

Preheat oven to 350°F. Parboil carrots and yams in lightly salted water until not quite tender. Drain vegetables and prunes. Layer carrots, yams, prunes, and apples in a casserole dish, sprinkling layers with sugar, salt, and pepper, and dotting with schmaltz. Pour I cup water into the casserole dish, cover and bake for 30 minutes or until apples are tender. Uncover and bake for about 5 minutes or until top is lightly browned. Serve hot as an accompaniment to main dish.

Hot Fruit Compote

This is a recipe where you can express your individuality. It's almost impossible to make it turn out wrong. Use almost any kind of fruit or nuts; leave out the nuts and raisins; add coconut or macaroon crumbs; be inventive. Fruit Compote is a wonderful buffet dish because it still tastes good when it cools off and it provides an alternative for the calorie counters who are so strong-willed they won't even taste your chocolate cake. You should be so lucky — that way you might have cake left over.

I can (I lb) sliced peaches, drained, juice reserved
I can (I lb) sliced pears, drained, juice reserved
$^1/_2$ lb dried, pitted prunes
$^1/_2$ lb dried apricots
I cup raisins
I cup slivered almonds
$^1/_2$ tsp cinnamon
$^1/_4$ tsp ground nutmeg
$^1/_2$ cup brandy
2 tbsp fresh lemon juice or to taste
4 tbsp dark brown sugar
(serves 8)

Preheat oven to 350°F. Layer fruit in a 4-pt casserole dish. Scatter raisins and almonds over fruit. Sprinkle with cinnamon and nutmeg. Place brandy and lemon juice in cup measure. Stir in brown sugar until dissolved. Pour over fruit. Add enough reserved fruit juice to just cover fruit. Bake for 30 minutes or until heated through.

Mohn Strudel

Time was when making strudel at home was too difficult, even for a good cook! But now filo dough is available in the freezer section of most supermarkets so strudel can be made easily at home — and it tastes better than store-bought. It's easier to make than you think. Try it!

---

3 cups poppy seed
$^3/_4$ cup granulated sugar
1 cup milk
2 tbsp grated lemon rind
$^1/_2$ cup raisins
12 filo leaves
$^1/_2$ cup butter, melted
confectioners' (icing) sugar for sprinkling
(serves 8–10)

Preheat oven to 375°F. Grease baking sheet and set aside. Place first 5 ingredients in saucepan and cook over low heat until thickened. Set aside. Unfold filo leaves and place between damp kitchen towels. Remove 1 leaf and place on dry kitchen towel. Brush with melted butter. Top with second leaf and brush with butter. Repeat with remaining leaves. Spoon poppy seed mixture down center of filo leaves to within 2 inches of long sides of pastry. Lift pastry in towel and roll, jelly-roll fashion. Brush seam with water and press gently to seal. Roll strudel onto prepared baking sheet, seam side down. Brush top and sides with melted butter. Bake for 35 to 40 minutes or until golden brown. Place baking sheet on wire rack to cool slightly. Remove strudel to serving dish, dust with confectioners' sugar, and serve warm.

Honey Cake

Honey Cake tastes best if made 24 hours before you serve it. Make it in any shape; glaze or leave plain; add nuts, raisins, or citron — or don't. It is traditional for the Jewish New Year and good at any time of year.

---

3 1/2 cups all-purpose (plain) flour
1 cup firmly packed dark brown sugar
1 tbsp baking powder
1 tsp baking soda
2 tsp cinnamon
1/2 tsp each ground allspice, nutmeg, ginger, and salt
4 eggs
1 3/4 cups honey
1 cup strong black coffee
4 tbsp vegetable oil or melted butter
1 cup coarsely chopped nuts
(makes 2 loaf cakes)

Preheat oven to 350°F. Grease and flour two 9 x 5-inch loaf pans and set aside. Place dry ingredients in large bowl and stir until well combined. Make well in center, add eggs, honey, coffee, and oil, and stir until smooth. Lightly flour nuts and stir into batter. Divide batter between prepared pans and bake for 1 hour or until toothpick inserted into center of cakes comes out clean. Cool in pans on wire rack for 10 minutes. Remove from pans and cool completely on wire rack.

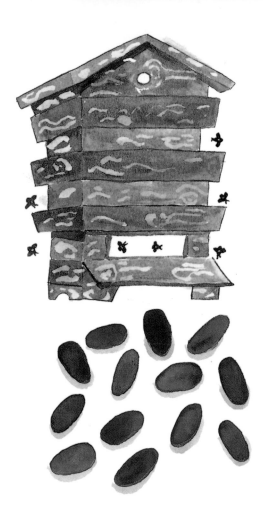

Teiglach

On Rosh Hashonah, the Jewish New Year, it is traditional to eat sweets, particularly honey. Honey Cake (see page 54) and apples dipped in honey are nice, but Teiglach (honey-dipped cookies) are special. Sweets for the New Year portend a sweet new year — or so one hopes. And what could taste better than a little honey — at any time!

2 cups honey
2 cups sugar
I tbsp ground ginger
3 eggs, beaten
I tbsp sugar
2 tbsp vegetable oil
2 cups sifted all-purpose (plain) flour
I tsp finely ground almonds
I tsp ground ginger
¼ tsp salt (optional)
(makes about 30)

Combine first 3 ingredients in saucepan and set aside. Place eggs, sugar, and oil in large bowl and beat well. Combine remaining ingredients and work into egg mixture to form soft dough. Flour hands, break off pieces of dough, and roll into ½ inch thick ropes. Cut ropes into ½ inch lengths. Bring honey mixture to a boil and drop in pieces of dough, a few at a time. Cover and simmer for 30 minutes. Stir gently with wooden spoon to bring cookies on bottom to surface. Cook until they are lightly browned, and dry and crisp inside. Remove with slotted spoon and place on waxed paper, not touching, until cool.

Almond Macaroons

Almond Macaroons are particularly popular at Passover, but why wait for Passover? They are good at any time of year. You may have difficulty making them if the weather is humid so wait for a dry, sunny day.

---

1 ²/₃ cups finely ground almonds
²/₃ cup sugar
grated rind of 2 lemons
4 egg whites
¹/₂ tsp almond extract
(makes about 30)

Preheat oven to 350°F. Line 2 baking sheets with aluminum (tin) foil and set aside. Place ground almonds, sugar, and lemon rind in large bowl and stir until well combined. Beat egg whites until almost stiff. Add almond extract and beat until stiff but not dry. Fold beaten egg whites into almond mixture. Spoon mixture into pastry (piping) bag fitted with large open star-shaped tip (8). Pipe 1 ¹/₂ inch rosettes onto prepared baking sheets about 1 inch apart. Bake for 20 minutes or until lightly browned, reversing position of baking sheets halfway through baking to ensure all cookies bake evenly. Slide aluminum foil onto wire racks and let stand for about 5 minutes. Peel macaroons off foil and return them to racks until completely cooled.

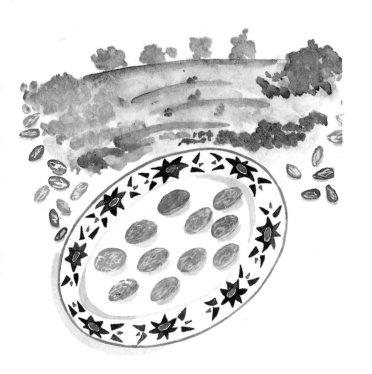

Index